ICECREAM MAKER COOKBOOK FOR BEGINNERS

From Novice To Ninja: Master The Art Of Homemade Ice Cream.Step-By-Step Instructions For Crafting Delicious Ice Cream With Your Favorite Appliance.

Melissa Trifordes

D1522019

Contents

INTRODUCTION:

If you're an ice cream lover but you love to eat homemade special ice cream than this book is all about you. Basically this is a cook book for "NINJA CREAMI". Now a day's ninja creami is worldwide famous for its taste and the techniques that machine uses. This is not just an ordinary ice cream maker this machine consists of some many advanced systems and techniques not only this people are loving and purchasing quickly as this machine makes creamier and most delicious ice-cream with simple easy steps.

The main question is what really Ninja Creami does? So with the stroke of a button, the Ninja Creami turns frozen solid bases into ice cream, sorbets, milkshakes, and more. The Creami can quickly transform a uniformly frozen block into an amazingly smooth, creamy texture, all thanks to Ninja's Creamy technology which not only enhance the taste of your ice cream but all increases the creaminess, texture quantity.

The ninja creami is different from the all the available blenders yes they are like blenders but with a highly advanced technology of a Creamify. This machine consists of The Creami machine and 2 pints. Although the Creami Machine is a big like any other machine, but it did fit on the kitchen counter well. It's somewhat higher but around the same size as an espresso machine. It also includes a cookbook and a quick start manual in addition to the appliance itself. The ice cream mix needs to sit in the freezer for at least 24 hours, which is something important that people discovered about the machine when they read the fast start guide briefly.

So the question is how to use this special ice-cream maker machine? Well than your answer is here. Fill the pints with the ice cream or sorbet combination you intend to use, then place them in the freezer for 24 hours to prepare the creami. When the mixture is frozen and you're ready to make ice cream, just remove the top of the pint, insert it inside the blender, and secure it. The computer will handle the rest of the process after you choose the mode. You will enjoy freshly made ice cream when the Creami shuts off after about 3 to 4 minutes! This is where you can add any mix-ins, such as candy or frozen fruit, before pressing the mix-in button to combine it with the ice cream.

RECIPES

CHOCOLATE PROTEIN ICE-CREAM:

For this all you need is this:

INGREDIENTS:

- Chocolate Fair Life Protein Shake
- Almond milk
- Chocolate pudding powder
- Sweetener
- Rainbow Sprinkles

COOKING TIME: 5 minutes

DIRECTIONS:

Use hand immersion blender to blend all ingredients minus sprinkles than carefully put this in pint container and freeze than for 24 hours. After this the main and important task is to spin on sorbet carefully just add a splash of almond milk so that it will blend well after that RE-SPIN, add sprinkles as many as you want than enjoy your chocolate protein ice-cream at home.

EGGNOG ICE-CREAM-GELATO:

They are quite rich flavor so they aren't available easily. This ice-cream is available only in holiday seasons like Easter, Christmas and Thanksgiving. They are expensive too just like flavors so by the help of Ninja Creami we can make this recipe easily at home and enjoy this by freezing them for later. The really nice thing about this recipe that it's mainly one ingredient recipe.

For this all you need is this:

INGREDIENTS:

- Commercial Eggnog from your favourite brand

DIRECTIONS:

The main thing about this recipe is that you just have to buy the eggnog from the part and store it in the NINGA CREAMI PINT CONTAINER. The final texture of the eggnog gelato is so incredibly smooth and creamy because of the amount of fat and dairy in the eggnog; it's truly difficult to imagine that something this good is so simple to create for your loved ones and for your special occasions.

- In a pint-sized Ninja Creami container that is empty, pour eggnog. For 24 hours, place the cover on and freeze.
- Take the pint out of the freezer 24 hours after freezing it. Take the cover off.
- Insert the pint into the outer basin. Turn the Ninja Creami machine while inserting the outer bowl with the pint. The outer bowl should lock into place. By pressing the GELATO button. The ice cream will combine and thicken up during the gelato process.
- After the GELATO function is finished, rotate the outer bowl and remove it from the Ninja Creami device. Make a hole along the middle, add a spoonful of eggnog or milk, and then re-spin the eggnog if it is crumbly or dry.

- If your machine doesn't have a gelato setting, you can still produce Ninja Creami Eggnog Ice Cream by processing ice cream. Even while it might not be quite as thick and creamy, the outcome will still be fantastic.)
- It's time to taste your ice cream! Enjoy!

PINEAPPLE SORBET:

INGREDIENTS:

- You only need Pineapple juice/can/pieces here as you have to store it overnight for the cubes

DIRECTIONS:

Fill the pint to the top with canned pineapple in juice, not water. This is crucial because ice would be too tough on the Creami blades and could shatter them.

Therefore, then filled the pint to the top of the fill line with canned pineapple pieces and juice (approximately 3/4 of a 20oz can), covered it, and placed it in the freezer overnight. The pineapple will be completely frozen the following day since you will throw it in the blender, set the setting to "sorbet," and wonderfully smooth sorbet came so delicious. So, it's a good thing you will follow the maximum fill line since else it probably wouldn't have worked. The sorbet eventually rose to the top of the pint. Creamy and delectable sorbet was produced! Success! Here your first recipe was made easily within minutes.

REGULAR VANILLA ICE CREAM:

For this all you need is this:

COOKING TIME: 5 minutes

INGREDIENTS:

- Oatmeal in (case you are not having cream)
- Milk (any) ALMOND would make it awesome
- Cream
- Vanilla Essence
- Chunks
- Sprinkles

DIRECTIONS:

The next thing you are supposed to do is to freeze cream/oatmeal/ together in a freezer for at least 24 hours. Put it in the Creami after chilling it for the night and spun it on ice-cream. You will feel some crumbliness in your ice-cream, and it will turn out so flakier just like Dippin' Dots. It will almost icier (similar to Halo Top and those other light ice creams). While it didn't turn out looking like typical and ordinary ice cream, it tasted fairly good. So better results mixed them with some Reese's Pieces and chunks than ran it through the mixer. If then serving, serve with some sprinkles and chunks that will increase more it's taste and this will be going to be the delicious easy prep vanilla ice-cream at home with Ninja.

RASPBERRY CHOCOLATE ICE-CREAM TRUFFLE:

INGREDIENTS:

- Raspberries cut in half
- Chocolate truffle (White)
- White chocolate
- Milk
- Heavy whipping cream
- Cream cheese

DIRECTIONS:

White chocolate and raspberries are a perfect match! Use your Ninja Creami to make raspberry white chocolate truffle ice cream right away! A light, not overly sweet raspberry ice cream serves as the foundation for this ice cream. Fresh raspberries and white chocolate truffles are the add-ins. Since white chocolate has a moderate flavor and a very smooth texture and raspberries have a somewhat sour flavor, the two flavors complement one another very well. So just spin around Ninja creami with these ingredients. If you are extra cream lover than you can use the function of the re-spin where you can have creamy textured ice-cream. Use re-spin function on spun ice cream only. Avoid using re-spin if the ice cream has already been frozen and spun. Rather, follow the original procedure (ice cream, gelato, etc.)

- In a mixing bowl, mash together the cream cheese, sugar, and raspberry jam.
- Combine everything with a whisk until well-combined and the sugar begins to dissolve.
- Pour in the milk and heavy cream. Stir everything up thoroughly while whisking. Due to how   thick the raspberry preserves mixture is, this may take a minute or two.
- Stir in 1/2 of the cut-in-half raspberries. Depending on their size, this will amount to 6–8 raspberries.

- Pour into a pint-sized Ninja Creami container that is empty and freeze for 24 hours after adding all the ingredients (apart from the mix-ins).
- Take the pint out of the freezer after 24 hours has passed. Take the cover off.
- Now the outside bowl goes the Ninja Creami. While inserting the outer bowl with the pint, turn the Ninja Creami machine. The outer bowl need to secure itself. Utilize the ICE CREAM button. During the ice cream function, the ice cream will combine and become wonderfully creamy.
- After the ice cream function is complete, rotate the outer bowl and remove it from the Ninja Creami.
- Cut a hole through the centre of the ice cream using a spoon, working from top to bottom. The mix-ins fill in this gap. Include 3 white chocolate truffles and 1/4 cup of raspberries.
- Rotate the outer bowl and take it out of the Ninja Creami after the ice cream feature is finished.
- Using a spoon, poke a hole through the centre of the ice cream from top to bottom. This hole is filled by the mix-ins. 3 white chocolate truffles and 1/4 cup of raspberries should be included. Make sure to carefully chop the raspberries and truffles in half.
- Reinstall the outer bowl and pint into the Ninja Creami machine and secure it. Select the MIX-IN option.
- Remove the outer bowl from the Ninja Creami when the MIX-IN cycle is finished.
- It's time to devour your ice cream! Enjoy!

NINJA CREAMI BROWNIE COOKIE ICE-CREAM:

INGREDIENTS:

- Heavy cream
- Milk
- Cream Cheese
- Sugar
- Vanilla Extract
- Little Debbie brownie
- Chocolate chip cookies
- Caramel chips
- Skor chips
- Caramel syrup

DIRECTIONS:

- In a bowl suitable for the microwave, soften the cream cheese for 10 seconds.
- The softened cream cheese should be combined with the sugar and vanilla using a whisk.
- Slowly pour in the milk and continue whisking until all ingredients are combined.
- Pour into a pint-sized Ninja Creami container. Place in freezer for at least 24 hours.
- Take the pint out of the freezer after 24 hours and put it in the outer bowl.
- On the Ninja Creami, press the ICE CREAM button.
- Chop the brownie and cookies into small pieces while the ice cream is processing.
- Remove the Ninja Creami's outer bowl once the ice cream has done processing.
- The brownie, cookies, chips, and syrup should be placed in the centre of the ice cream, which should be a 1 1/2-inch hole.
- Select the MIX-IN method and place the pint back into the Ninja Creami.

- After the MIX-IN procedure is finished, take the food out of the machine and serve.
- Now your brownie ice-cream is ready enjoy and serve them.

VANILLA BEAN ICE-CREAM:

You can make a variety of other favourite ice cream flavors using this vanilla bean ice cream foundation recipe! To make a fruity strawberry ice cream, add fruit. The greatest chocolate chip ice cream will have chocolate chips added. For the best taffy apple ice cream, combine apples and caramel. There are countless possibilities.

INGREDIENTS:

- Vanilla Bean Paste

  For this recipe, vanilla bean paste should be used because it gives the ice cream a richer flavour. However, you can use vanilla extract if you don't have access to vanilla bean paste. The vanilla bean paste and vanilla extract are mixed in a 1:1 ratio.

- Cream Cheese

  Make sure the cream cheese is at room temperature before combining it with the other ingredients. The cream cheese can be softened if necessary by microwaving it for 5 to 10 seconds. For this dish, you can either use standard or low-fat cream cheese.

- Milk

  You can substitute lower-fat milk or a non-dairy option like oat milk, coconut milk, or almond milk for the whole milk I used.

- Sugar

  Depending on how sweet you prefer your ice cream, feel free to add more or less sugar. Utilize the LITE ICE CREAM function as opposed to the ICE CREAM function if you opt to use a sugar replacement, such as monk fruit or agave sweeteners.

- Heavy whipping cream

Feel free to reduce or increase the sugar based on how sweet you would like the ice cream. If you decide to use a sugar substitute, such as monk fruit or agave sweeteners, use the LITE ICE CREAM function instead of the ICE CREAM function.

DIRECTIONS:

- Cream cheese, sugar, and vanilla bean paste should all be combined in one bowl. Stir together with a whisk until everything is well blended and the sugar begins to dissolve.
- Add the milk and heavy whipping cream. Stir everything up thoroughly while whisking.
- Place the ingredients in a pint-sized Ninja Creami container that is empty and freeze for a full day.
- Take the pint out of the freezer after 24 hours has passed. Take the cover off.
- In the outer bowl, put the pint of Ninja Creami. Turn the Ninja Creami machine while inserting the outer bowl with the pint. The outer bowl should lock into place. Make use of the ICE CREAM button. The ice cream will blend together and get incredibly creamy throughout the ice cream function.
- Turn the outer bowl and remove it from the Ninja Creami machine after the ice cream operation has finished.
- It's time to devour your ice cream! Enjoy!

CREAMI BANANA CHOCOLATE COOKIE LITE ICE-CREAM:

Everyone will adore this light and creamy ice cream! Mostly bananas—just bananas—make up the basis. The flavor and texture of this cooling ice cream are enhanced by the fresh fruit. Since the recipe calls for mashing the bananas before adding them to the pint container, it is advised to use fresh bananas. If frozen bananas are used, they must first be thawed so that they may be mashed up before the pint is frozen.

INGREDIENTS:

- Bananas
  bananas that have just been picked and mashed. Bananas that have been frozen can be utilized; however, they must first be thawed and mashed before being added to the Ninja Creami pint container.
- Almond milk
  This recipe called for almond milk with a toasted coconut taste, but you could use any flavour of almond (or other nut) milk. After adding the bananas to the pint, pour enough liquid to reach the maximum fill line.
- Chocolate chips
  You can use milk chocolate, dark chocolate, micro, or large chocolate chips. If you don't have chocolate chips, you can substitute a broken-up chocolate bar or magic shell chocolate syrup

DIRECTIONS:

- In the Creami Pint, mash three ripe bananas.
- Fill the container to the top with Toasted Coconut Almond milk.
- For at least 12 hours, freeze.
- Insert the Ninja Creami pint into the outside bowl of the Ninja Creami machine.
- Process Lite Ice Cream and repeat the process twice.
- with chocolate chips Make a 1 ½- inch wide hole in the pint's bottom, add the chocolate chips, and stir with the Mix In. Enjoy!

CREAMI BOOZY CHERRY GARCIA ICE-CREAM:

INGREDIENTS:

- Vanilla Pudding Mix

You can make your own if you don't have instant vanilla pudding mix. We came up this recipe for DIY Instant Vanilla Pudding Mix.

- Milk

For this dish, whole milk was used. Although milk with a lower fat content is an option, the final product might not be as rich and creamy as milk with a higher fat content. If you'd rather, you can substitute regular half and half for lactose-free half and half.

- Cherry Whiskey

You can skip the whiskey or substitute bourbon, black rum, or brandy. The flavour will depend on the type of alcohol you use.

- Cherries

This dish called for black lack cherries. You have a choice between frozen or fresh cherries. If you don't have any fresh or frozen cherries, you may alternatively use jarred maraschino cherries, although they are considerably sweeter and taste more like sugar.

- Chocolate chip

Any type of chocolate chips will do in this recipe. Therefore, you can use a chocolate bar if that's all you have. You can use chocolate chips of any size or shape. As long as the fragments are tiny enough to be broken down during the mixing procedure.

Directions:

- In a bowl, whisk the first four ingredients together until thoroughly incorporated and the mixture has begun to thicken.

- Pour into a pint Ninja Creami container, and then freeze for at least 24 hours on a level surface
- Process in the Ninja Creami using the Ice Cream setting.
- Remove the pint from the machine, then drill a hole through the ice cream to the bottom of the container.
- Put the cherries in after adding the pint to the Creami.
- Use the mix-ins process to process.
- Clear a hole to the bottom of the ice cream in the container after removing the pint from the machine.
- Refill the Creami with the pint after adding the chocolate chips.
- Using the mix-ins method of processing.
- Enjoy!

INGREDIENTS:

- Egg yolks

For this dish, big eggs were used. Approximately 14 cup of egg yolks is equal to 4 large egg yolks. Use 14 cup of egg yolks in total if you use a different-sized egg.

- Corn syrup

This recipe called for light corn syrup, which was utilised. The flavour of the gelato will be significantly altered if black corn syrup is used, hence it is not advised. Light corn syrup can be replaced with agave nectar or honey.

- Granulated sugar

For this recipe, regular sugar was used. You can substitute any other sweetener you choose. Depending on the sugar replacement you use, a different amount will be required, and the outcome will change.

- Heavy Cream

You can substitute milk and butter for heavy cream if you don't have any on hand. Mix 14 cup of melted butter with 34 cup of milk to make 1 cup of heavy cream. Completely combine.

- Milk

For this dish, whole milk was used. Although milk with a lower fat content is an option, the final product might not be as rich and creamy as milk with a higher fat content.

- Pumpkin Puree

The simplest choice for this recipe's pumpkin puree is canned pumpkin puree. However, you may use cooked sweet potatoes, cooked butternut squash, or fresh pumpkin if you don't have any on hand. To get a smooth texture, just make sure the ingredient is boiled, all seeds and skins are removed, and it is thoroughly blended.

- Apple pie spice extract and pumpkin pie spice extract are both options.
- Nutmeg

Adding extra nutmeg is optional. You can therefore omit this ingredient if you don't have any.

DIRECTIONS:

- In a saucepan, mash together the egg yolks with the sugar and corn syrup. Whisk the ingredients together thoroughly.
- Add the milk, nutmeg, pumpkin pie spice, pumpkin pie extract, and pumpkin puree (optional). Stir constantly until everything is thoroughly incorporated.
- In a medium-sized saucepan, cook the ingredients. Stir the mixture constantly until it registers 165 degrees Fahrenheit on an instant-read thermometer.
- Turn off the stove, step 4. Once the mixture has been taken off the heat, pour it into a pint-sized Ninja Creami container after passing it through a mesh strainer.
- Cool the pint container by dipping it into a bowl of ice water.
- Place the pint container's lid on top, then freeze it for 24 hours.
- Take the pint out of the freezer and take the top off after 24 hours.
- Put a pint in the outside bowl and put the Ninja Creami machine to work.
- Select the gelato method.
- Remove the pint from the Ninja Creami once the procedure is finished.
- Enjoy after serving!

INGREDIENTS:

- Milk

Reduced-fat milk was used for this recipe for chocolate milk. You can choose to use full-fat milk or a non-dairy milk alternative like oat or nut milk if you'd like.

- Coffee syrup

Syrup was utilized, and it was of the Autocrat brand. If you don't have access to this brand, you can use a different flavour or brand instead. Brew coffee is not a good substitute because it will result in a significantly icier final product due to the higher water content.

- Creamer

This recipe called for caramel almond creamer of the Good and Gather brand. Use any creamer you like, regardless of flavour or brand. Regular creamer can be used with a small amount of caramel flavouring if you don't have caramel creamer on hand.

- Oreos

Because they have additional cream in the cookie, Oreos (or a store-brand cookie) are highly recommended for this recipe. If Oreos aren't your thing, you can substitute any other cookie you like, although the texture can be different.

DIRECTIONS:

- Mix together the chocolate milk, coffee syrup, and Ninja Creami pint.
- the remaining space in the container with the caramel creamer.
- 24 hours of covering and freezing
- Remove the pint from the freezer after 24 hours, add it to the outer bowl, and then add the Ninja Creami. Select the ICE CREAM procedure.

- Take the ice cream out of the freezer after the procedure is finished, take off the lid, and then use a spoon to cut a 1.5-inch hole in the centre of the ice cream. Insert three of the smashed Oreo cookies into the hole.
- Place the pint into the outer bowl, replace the lid on it, and then re-start the Ninja Creami. Select MIX IN as the setting.
- The other 3 crumbled Oreos should be placed on top of the ice cream in the bowl. Enjoy!

CREAMI BANANA PUDDING ICE-CREAM

INGREDIENTS:

- Cream Cheese

Before using, ensure that the cream cheese is at room temperature. In the absence of such, it will probably be clumpy. You can use low-fat or regular.

- Extract of vanilla

The recipe called for vanilla extract, however vanilla paste can also be used.

- Heavy Cream

On occasion, heavy cream might leave a buttery or greasy taste on the back of the spoon. Overmixing the ice cream may result in this. In essence, the butter is made from the heavy cream. You can substitute 12 and 12 for the heavy cream to stop this from happening.

- Milk

Whole milk was used; however, any type of milk or dairy alternative may be utilised.

Make sure to purchase banana cream instant pudding and not the cook-and-serve variety.

- Bananas

Make this recipe with fresh bananas. The dish becomes creamier and sweeter thanks to the bananas.

- Nutmeg

Alternatives like ginger, cinnamon, and cloves work well.

- Cinnamon

Good alternatives include cinnamon, nutmeg, cloves, and ginger.

- A Nilla Wafer

As a substitute for Nilla Wafers, you can use any of your favourite cookies.

DIRECTIONS:

- One banana, heavy cream, milk, pudding mix, and cream cheese should all be thoroughly blended in a blender.
- The second banana should be taken, mashed, and added to the Ninja Creami pint.
- Add a dash of cinnamon and nutmeg after pouring the liquid mixture into the Ninja Creami pint.
- For 24 hours, freeze the pint container with the lid on.
- Take the pint out of the freezer once it has frozen, then put it into the outer dish.
- Process by selecting the "Ice cream" button.
- When finished, take out the pint and carve a 1-inch tunnel through the middle of the ice
- Process by selecting the "Mix-ins" button.
- Crumble 1 Nilla Wafer and 1 Nilla Wafer on top before serving. Enjoy!

INGREDIENTS:

- Coconut Cream

use canned coconut cream, which you can find in the grocery store's canned food section. In most cases, it is near the ethnic food section. The final texture will be less creamy and icier if you use coconut milk from the cooler part of the grocery store.

- Pineapple

I like to use canned "tidbits" because they are more convenient and always available. You can substitute fresh pineapple if you'd like. Just make sure the pieces are the right sizes before adding them to the pint container. that you bite-size the fresh pineapple

- Coconut

Use either sweetened or unsweetened coconut. I like to use toasted coconut since it gives the ice cream a great nutty flavour. You may purchase toasted coconut or create your own by cooking it for about 3 minutes over medium heat in a skillet.

- Rum

didn't use rum in this recipe, but you can use whatever kind of rum or coconut rum you choose. Do not add more than one ounce of rum to the mixture if you want to add it before freezing. The combination might not completely freeze if you add extra rum.

DIRECTIONS:

- An empty Ninja Creami pint container should be filled with coconut cream and pineapple before being frozen for 24 hours. It doesn't need to be stirred before freezing.
- Take the pint out of the freezer after 24 hours has passed. Take the cover off.

- In the outer bowl, put the pint of Ninja Creami. Turn the Ninja Creami machine while inserting the outer bowl with the pint. The outer bowl should lock into place. To make lite ice cream, press the button. The ice cream will blend together and get really creamy during the lite ice cream function.
- When the lite ice cream feature is finished, spin the outer bowl and remove it from the Ninja Creami device.
- Make a hole through the centre of the ice cream from top to bottom using a spoon. You will put the mix-ins in this hole. Add 1 tablespoon of sliced pineapple and 1 tablespoon of toasted coconut.
- Reinstall the outer bowl and pint into the Ninja Creami machine and secure it. Select the MIX-IN option.
- Remove the outer bowl from the Ninja Creami when the MIX-IN cycle is finished.
- It's time to devour your ice cream! Enjoy!

INGREDIENTS:

- Pineapple

  This dish calls for crushed pineapple that has been canned and put in thick syrup. As an alternative, use pineapple bits or chunks. The final product won't be as sweet or creamy if you choose to use pineapple juice or light syrup\p

- Whipped coconut

  In this recipe, Coco Lopez was used, however any brand of sweetened cream of coconut or Coco Real can be used instead.

- Coconut

  It's possible to utilize coconut that has been sweetened or not. The coconut can either be mixed in or used as a final garnish before serving the sorbet.

- Creamer for Almond Milk

  Silk Sweet and Creamy This recipe called for almond milk creamer. Any brand may be used, but keep in mind that it is CREAMER and not milk that is utilised.

DIRECTIONS:

- Stirring is necessary after adding all the contents to the pint container, excluding the shredded coconut.
- The top should be flattened, covered, and frozen for 24 hours.
- Take out of the freezer. Allow the container to stand outside for 10 minutes at room temperature before spinning.
- Put the pint container in the outer bowl and the Ninja Creami machine on top of it.
- Select the sorbet procedure and start the machine.
- Use the Sorbet method to spin.

- Adding coconut mix-ins or removing the sorbet from the Ninja Creami after the sorbet-making procedure is finished are both optional. If you want to use coconut as a mix-in, make a little tunnel along the centre of the sorbet and pour the coconut in. Put the pint container in the outer bowl of the Ninja Creami and turn it on. Opt for the mix-ins feature. Scoop and enjoy once the procedure is finished!
- It's time to taste your sorbet!

Smoothie bowls are quite trendy right now! Smoothie bowls resemble the standard smoothie that you usually have for breakfast, a snack, or throughout the day. The numerous fantastic toppings that can be added to a smoothie bowl are the primary distinction between it and a smoothie. The fantastic toppings can't be added to smoothies because they are normally consumed with a straw. The fact that you can tailor each and every component in smoothie bowls to your preferences is absolutely fantastic. Simply by choosing which ingredients to include in your smoothie bowl, you may make it as nutritious or as unhealthy as you wish.

In order to make this smoothie bowl, we included a few breakfast staples including coffee and bananas. Breakfast smoothie bowl that is incredibly thick and silky is the end result! Making smoothie bowls is a fantastic method to clean up the refrigerator because you can add almost anything you want to them. Almost any fruit or vegetable can be added, and frequently the smoothie bowl's vegetables are undetectable.

INGREDIENTS:

- Coffee

This recipe works with freshly brewed or already-made coffee or iced coffee. Use the same coffee mix you would typically use to make a cup of coffee.

- Acorn Milk

For this recipe, any kind of milk will work. If preferred, coffee creamer can also be used.

- Espresso Almond Butter

Use the nut butter of your choice if you like. The mocha almond butter I used was a little on the sweeter side and had a hint of chocolate flavour. Use your preferred!

- Raspberries

It's best to use fresh berries. Raspberries could be replaced with strawberries, blueberries, or blackberries.

- Banana

  You can increase the amount of berries in this recipe in place of the bananas if you don't like the flavour of bananas.

- Toppings

  Banana, Raspberry, Strawberry, Sliced Almonds

  Espresso Beans with Chocolate Coating

  Maple or honey syrup

DIRECTIONS:

- Blend all ingredients in a blender until they are completely smooth.
- Pour into a Ninja Creami pint container that is empty, and then freeze for 24 hours.
- Take the pint out of the freezer after 24 hours has passed. Take the cover off.
- In the outer bowl, put the pint of Ninja Creami. Turn the Ninja Creami machine while inserting the outer bowl with the pint. The outer bowl should lock into place. Activate the Smoothie button. The components will combine and become extremely creamy during the smoothie function.
- When the smoothie function is finished, spin the outer bowl and remove it from the Ninja Creami device.
- In a bowl, scoop the smoothie. drizzle with honey or maple syrup. Add raspberries, chocolate-covered coffee beans, sliced bananas, and nut slices on top.
- It's time to consume your smoothie bowl! Add your preferred toppings, then enjoy!

Gelato is typically created using an egg-based formula. There are no eggs because this recipe is for VEGAN gelato. You're undoubtedly wondering how the heck we managed to manufacture gelato without using eggs. Well, it got a little difficult at first, but I eventually found a very fantastic post on Food Nouveau that broke down the instructions for creating VEGAN gelato. To make it taste like peanut butter, I changed the original recipe.

The outcomes were outstanding! The flavour was strong and the texture was quite rich and creamy.

INGREDIENTS:

- Unsweetened Full

Almond milk, cashew milk, or any other beloved dairy-free milk alternative can be substituted in place of the fat coconut milk (canned). Since canned coconut milk is thick and creamy and gives the gelato a nice texture, I really enjoy using it.

- Sugar

Since there isn't much sugar in this dish, I wouldn't advise doing away with it entirely. The sugar gives the gelato sweetness and gives it a creamy texture. A sugar substitute should not be used in this recipe.

- Cornstarch: no alternatives

Use your preferred nut butter instead of peanut butter. Almond, cashew, or walnut butter all work well. Even gritty nut butters are OK!

- Vegan Dark Chocolate Peanut Butter Cups (Cut into Eighths) – Since they are vegan, I used dark chocolate peanut butter cups that are NOT REAL. You can use any vegan candy you prefer as long as you cut them into little pieces to ensure a smooth gelato mixture.
- Any nut may be substituted for peanuts (chopped). To ensure that they blend in properly, chop them into small pieces.

DIRECTIONS:

- Combine the coconut milk, sugar, and corn starch in a small pot. Cook while continuously whisking over medium heat. Cook the mixture until it begins to boil. Turn the heat to low once the mixture boils and let it simmer for 3–4 minutes.
- Turn off the heat, then stir in the peanut butter.
- Transfer to an empty Ninja Creami pint container and freeze for 24 hours.
- Afterwards, take the pint out of the freezer. Take the cover off.
- In the outer bowl, put the pint of Ninja Creami. Turn the Ninja Creami machine while inserting the outer bowl with the pint. The outer bowl should lock into place. Make use of the gelato button. The mixture will combine and get quite creamy during the gelato process.
- When the gelato feature is finished, spin the outer bowl and remove it from the Ninja Creami device.
- Make a hole through the centre of the gelato from top to bottom using a spoon. You will put the mix-ins in this hole. Add the chopped peanuts and dark chocolate peanut butter cups. Make sure the peanut butter cups are broken up into small bits. You should make sure that these mix-ins are in fairly small bits because the mix-in function will not break them into smaller pieces.
- Reinstall the outer bowl and pint into the Ninja Creami machine and secure it. Select the MIX-IN option.
- Remove the outer bowl from the Ninja Creami when the MIX-IN cycle is finished.
- It's time to devour your gelato! Enjoy!

NINJA CREAMI PEANUT BUTTER BANANA ICE-CREAM

INGREDIENTS:

- This recipe calls for cream cheese; however Greek yoghurt or mascarpone cheese can be substituted if you don't have any. Depending on what is substituted, the flavour and texture may change.
- The recipe calls for cocoa powder, which is advised. Although hot chocolate mix can be used, the cocoa flavour won't be as potent.
- Any type of sugar or sugar replacement can be used with stevia.
- Raw agave nectar can be substituted with honey, maple syrup, and molasses.
- Banana liquor may be substituted for banana extract.
- Coconut Cream: Although coconut milk can be used, the final product can be less creamy.
- Almond milk may be substituted for other types of milk.
- Almond, cashew, or any other nut butter may be substituted for the peanut butter.
- Banana: Bananas enhance the flavour and creaminess of the dish. Anything else should not be used in place of the bananas.

DIRECTIONS:

- Melt the cream cheese in the microwave for 10 seconds using a bowl or blender cup that is microwave-safe.
- Blend the cream cheese with the remaining ingredients in a blender until thoroughly blended. Up until the maximum fill line, pour the mixture into a Ninja Creami pint. (I drank the remaining liquid, which was around 12 a cup)
- For 24 hours, freeze the pint with the lid on.
- Take the pint out of the freezer after 24 hours has passed.
- When choosing the "Lite Ice Cream" technique, pour the pint into the outer dish.
- When the processing is complete, serve and enjoy!

NINJA CREAMI CHOCOLATE PEANUT BUTTER BANANA ICE-CREAM

Before adding the ingredients to the Ninja Creami pint container, Ninja Creami Chocolate Peanut Butter Banana Ice Cream, make sure to thoroughly combine them in a mixer. For mixing, you can usually get away with either a spoon or a whisk. However, unless the other components are blended together, the cocoa powder does not integrate properly with them. Believe me. I made multiple attempts, but the cocoa powder always ends up sitting on top of the mixture. So get out that blender, add everything (except the mix-ins) to it, and blend until thoroughly blended. It should just take 3 to 4 seconds to complete. However, that extra time will be of the utmost importance!

INGREDIENTS:

- Cocoa Butter (Dark Cocoa Powder) In order to achieve a rich, powerful chocolate flavour in this recipe, I used dark cocoa powder. Although the flavour will be less potent, you can use normal cocoa powder.
- Equal Parts

You can substitute any nondairy product. Instead of half and half, you can, if necessary, use a mixture of heavy cream and milk. The use of half and half in place of heavy cream, however, I've discovered creates a better texture.

- Chocolate Chunks (or Chips)
- The chocolate chunks add substantial chocolate chunks to the entire batch of ice cream. Use chocolate chips or micro chocolate chips if you want the bits to be smaller. Use various flavored chips, such as caramel or white chocolate, if you want to experiment.
- Use fresh bananas for this dish if possible. The bananas give the dish a creamier texture and more sweetness.

- You can use either smooth or chunky peanut butter. You can choose to use almond, cashew, walnut, or another nut butter in place of the peanut butter if you'd like.

DIRECTIONS:

- Blend the following ingredients in a blender: bananas, peanut butter, chocolate powder, and half and half.
- Pour everything into a Ninja Creami Pint bottle.
- The pint container's lid should be on, and it should be frozen for 24 hours on a level surface. Take the pint out of the freezer after 24 hours has passed. Take the cover off.
- Take the pint out of the freezer after 24 hours has passed. Take the cover off.
- In the outer bowl, put the pint of Ninja Creami. Turn the Ninja Creami machine while inserting the outer bowl with the pint. The outer bowl should lock into place. Make use of the ICE CREAM button. The ice cream will blend together and get incredibly creamy throughout the ice cream function.
- Once more spin is required.
- The outer bowl should be turned and released from the Ninja Creami machine when the ice cream function has finished.
- Create a hole down the centre of the ice cream using a spoon. Once more inserting the pint into the Ninja Creami machine, add the chocolate chunks.
- Select the process and function for the "Mix-Ins. Take it out of the machine after processing is complete.
- You can enjoy your ice cream now! Enjoy!

NINJA CREAMI FROZEN HOT CHOCOLATE ICE-CREAM

INGREDIENTS:

- A chocolate milk
- For this dish, whole milk was used, however low-fat milk can also be utilised. Lower fat milk could result in a less creamy finished product.
- Equal Parts
  In the absence of half and half, you can substitute 3 parts whole milk and 1-part heavy cream.
- Hot Cocoa Blend
  Making your own hot cocoa mix is one option if none is available. Here is a recipe we discovered!
- Sweet and Creamy Silk Almond Milk Creamer This recipe called for almond milk creamer. Any brand may be used, but keep in mind that it is CREAMER and not milk that is utilized.

DIRECTIONS:

- In a medium bowl, mix the chocolate milk, half & half, and creamer.
- Heat the milk in the bowl in the microwave on high until it is warm but not boiling. (Roughly 2 minutes.)
- Add the hot chocolate packet's contents right away after removing from the microwave.
- Mix everything thoroughly by whisking. (Warming the milk first aids in blending the chocolate.)
- Mixture should be poured into Creami pint and given 10 minutes to cool in the fridge.
- Then, put the mixture in the freezer for 24 hours after giving it one more fast whisk.
- Place the pint container inside the Ninja Creami and set the machine to make ice cream.
- After the procedure is finished, take the pint out of the Ninja Creami device.
- If preferred, top with a sprinkle of small marshmallows when serving.

NINJA CREAMI ALMOND JOY ICE-CREAM

In this dish, every flavour present in an almond pleasure is combined. Ice cream made with coconut, chocolate, and almonds is delectable.

INGREDIENTS:

- For this recipe, whole milk was used, however lower fat milk can also be used. Chocolate milk Lower fat milk could result in a less creamy finished product.
- You can use 3 parts whole milk and 1-part heavy cream for half & half if you don't have any on hand.
- Creamer for Almond Milk, Silk Sweet and Creamy This recipe called for almond milk creamer. Any brand may be used, but keep in mind that it is CREAMER and not milk that is utilised.
- Vanilla extract may be substituted for almond extract if you don't have any. Although less potent, the flavour will be similar. Consequently, use almost twice as much vanilla if you do.
- Used in this recipe was cream of coconut from Coco Real. Use any kind of coconut cream, including Coco Lopez. This component can be skipped for a softer coconut flavour.
- Shredded coconut can be used in coconut-toasted dishes, whether it is sweetened or not. Untoasted can be used if you'd rather, however toasting is recommended.
- Almonds, sliced after toasting. Whole almonds are not advised for use in this recipe because they will be harder on the mixer and won't break up very much as they are mixed in.

DIRECTIONS:

- In a pint-sized Ninja Creami container, combine the ingredients.
- For 24 hours, freeze. In the freezer, make sure the pint container is level.
- Put the pint into the outer container after taking it out of the freezer after 24 hours. Put the ingredients in the Ninja Creami and process the ice cream.
- Once the procedure is finished, spin once again.

- The pint should be taken out of the Ninja Creami machine. Open the lid.
- Blend ins. Add coconut, almonds, and small chocolate chips that have been toasted (if desired). Refill the Ninja Creami with the ingredients and process using the mix-ins feature.
- If preferred, garnish the dish with a little toasted coconut and almonds. maybe some chocolate dipping sauce too!

NINJA CREAMI CHOCOLATE AND VANILLA ICE-CREAM

INGREDIENTS:

- Chocolate milk
- For this dish, whole milk was used, however low-fat milk can also be utilised. Lower fat milk could result in a less creamy finished product.
- Equal Parts
  In the absence of half and half, you can substitute 3 parts whole milk and 1-part heavy cream.
- Hot Cocoa Blend
  Making your own hot cocoa mix is one option if none is available. Here is a recipe we discovered!
- Sweet and Creamy Silk Almond Milk Creamer This recipe called for almond milk creamer. Any brand may be used, but keep in mind that it is CREAMER and not milk that is utilized
- Vanilla based creams
- Vanilla essence

DIRECTIONS:

- In a medium bowl, mix the chocolate milk, half & half, vanilla essence and vanilla creamer.
- Heat the milk in the bowl in the microwave on high until it is warm but not boiling. (Roughly 2 minutes.)Add the hot chocolate packet's contents right away after removing from the microwave.
- Mix everything thoroughly by whisking. (Warming the milk first aids in blending the chocolate.)Mixture should be poured into Creami pint and given 10 minutes to cool in the fridge.
- Then, put the mixture in the freezer for 24 hours after giving it one more fast whisk.
- Place the pint container inside the Ninja Creami and set the machine to make ice cream.
- After the procedure is finished, take the pint out of the Ninja Creami device.If preferred, top with a sprinkle of small marshmallows when serving.

NINJA CREAMI PEACHES AND CREAM ICE-CREAM

INGREDIENTS:

- Use one complete, fresh, huge peach. The container should be filled approximately halfway. You could therefore need to use 2 peaches, depending on the size of the peach. Peaches in cans are one option. I would advise purchasing sliced peaches though. Because I didn't use canned peaches for this recipe, I'm not sure how the syrup from the canned peaches would turn out. I'd advise draining the peaches before adding them to the pint jar.
- Use the creamer Natural Bliss Sweet Cream. Any brand may be used, or vanilla-flavored creamer may be substituted. No additional sugar was required because the creamer I used is already sweetened.
- You may probably need to add sweetness to taste if you choose a creamer that doesn't include a lot of sugar

DIRECTIONS:

- Cut a fresh peach into bits measuring 1 to 2 inches.
- Fill the pint container with peach chunks of Ninja Creami.
- dispense the creamer. You may need more or less than the suggested 1 cup, depending on the size of the peach you are using.
- Frozen for 24 hours with the lid on.
- Pull the pint out of the freezer after 24 hours. Lid removed.
- The outer bowl should be filled with the pint of Ninja Creami. Once it locks into place, insert the outer bowl with the pint into the Ninja Creami machine. Toggle the ICE CREAM button. Ice cream will combine and get extremely creamy during the ice cream function. Make it creamier if necessary by re-spinning.
- Turn the outer bowl and remove it from the Ninja Creami machine after the ice cream operation has finished.
- It's time to devour your ice cream! Enjoy!

INGREDIENTS:

- Watermelon

a fresh watermelon that has been seeded. Watermelon sherbet will taste better if it is more recent and sweeter.

- If you don't have sweetened condensed milk, you can make your own by adding sugar. Here is a recipe that demonstrates how to prepare it.
- Lime Juice

Both fresh and store-bought lime juice are excellent. You can substitute lemon or orange juice for lime juice if you don't have any on hand.

- Salt

The salt works to accentuate the watermelon's sweetness. You can, however, eliminate the salt if you'd like.

DIRECTIONS:

- Blend all ingredients in a blender until well-combined; this shouldn't take more than a few seconds.
- Transfer the mixture into a pint-sized Ninja Creami container. Place the pint container's lid on top, then freeze it for 24 hours.
- After the pint has frozen, take it out of the freezer and put it in the outer dish.
- Select and proceed with the "Sorbet" option.
- Spin the sherbet again to finish processing it.
- Take the pint out, then serve! Enjoy!

NINJA CREAMI LOW CALORIE CHOCOLATE CHEESECAKE

INGREDIENTS:

- Triangles of fat-free cheese made with Goat Cheese Creamy Light Cheese. Cream cheese can be substituted if you don't have this cheese.
- This recipe needs DARK cocoa powder, which is available online. The flavour of the chocolate is stronger thanks to this variation on conventional cocoa powder.
- Liquid saccharine: You can use any kind of sugar replacement in this recipe. Select your preferred!
- If you don't have xanthan gum, you can substitute 15 grams of cornstarch for it as long as you first produce a slurry and then heat it before adding it to the mixture.
- Water is required for this recipe, both hot and cold.

DIRECTIONS:

- To enhance the flavour and make the cocoa powder more chocolate-like, bloom it. In the pint tub, mix the hot water and chocolate powder together.
- Unwrap the cheese triangles and stir in the liquid saccharine (or other sugar substitute) when the cocoa powder has completely dissolved
- Make a thorough blending with an immersion blender.
- Blend in the xanthan gum after adding cold water up to the top line.
- Place the Ninja Creami Pint's lid on it and freeze it for twenty-four hours.
- Remove from the freezer after 24 hours, remove the lid, and put the food in the Ninja Creami outer bowl.
- Select and carry out the "Smoothie Bowl" process.
- Remove the pint from the outer bowl and serve as soon as the machine is completed processing! Enjoy!

INGREDIENTS:

- Egg yolks
  For this dish, big eggs were used. Approximately 14 cup of egg yolks is equal to 4 large egg yolks. Use 14 cup of egg yolks in total if you use a different-sized egg.
- This recipe called for light corn syrup, which was utilised. The flavour of the gelato will be significantly altered if black corn syrup is used, hence it is not advised. Light corn syrup can be replaced with agave nectar or honey.
- Granulated sugar

For this recipe, regular sugar was used. You can substitute any other sweetener you choose. Depending on the sugar replacement you use, a different amount will be required, and the outcome will change.

- Heavy Cream

If you don't have heavy cream, you can use butter and milk. Melted 1/4 cup butter and 3/4 cup milk are combined to form 1 cup of heavy cream. Combine well.

- This recipe called for whole milk, which was utilised. Even if milk with a reduced fat level is an option, the final product might not be as rich and creamy.
- It is not recommended to leave out or substitute butter flavour extract because it is necessary to obtain the butter pecan flavour.
- If you don't have pecans, you can substitute any other nut of your choice for the pecan pieces.

NINJA CREAMI PEACHES AND CREAM GELATO

INGREDIENTS:

- Instant oatmeal (Use 2 1.05 individual serving packages.) Oatmeal can be used in any taste or brand. Oatmeal should be prepared already or be instant.
- If you don't have buttery cinnamon roll seasoning (Flavor God), a mixture of vanilla, cinnamon, and honey works well as a stand-in.
- For this recipe, heavy cream powder (from Hoosier Hill Farm) is called for because heavy cream, which is a liquid, would result in a very different texture and flavour.
- Any yoghurt should be suitable for this recipe. For this recipe, you have the option of using plain, vanilla, or even peach-flavored. Adjust the flavour if you use oats with a different flavor.

DIRECTIONS:

- Add the boiling water to the small mixing bowl with the two packages of oatmeal. While it cools, let the oatmeal to set.
- Pour the oatmeal into a Ninja Creami pint container once it has cooled.
- Include yoghurt, cinnamon roll seasoning, and heavy cream powder.
- Combine thoroughly using a spoon or the Ninja Creami's milkshake function.
- Spend 24 hours freezing on a level surface.
- After the 24-hour period, take the pint out of the freezer and put it in the outer dish. Use the Gelato feature to process the addition in the Ninja Creami. Re-spin once for softer gelato.

INGREDIENTS:

- Egg yolks

For this dish, big eggs were used. Approximately 14 cup of egg yolks is equal to 4 large egg yolks. Use 14 cup of egg yolks in total if you use a different-sized egg.

- This recipe called for light corn syrup, which was utilised. The flavour of the gelato will be significantly altered if black corn syrup is used, hence it is not advised. Light corn syrup can be replaced with agave nectar or honey.
- Granulated sugar

For this recipe, regular sugar was used. You can substitute any other sweetener you choose. Depending on the sugar replacement you use, a different amount will be required, and the outcome will change.

- Heavy Cream: You can substitute milk and butter for heavy cream if you don't have any on hand. Mix 14 cup of melted butter with 34 cup of milk to make 1 cup of heavy cream. Completely combine.
- For this dish, whole milk was used. Although milk with a lower fat content is an option, the final product might not be as rich and creamy as milk with a higher fat content.
- The simplest choice for this recipe's pumpkin puree is canned pumpkin puree. However, you may use cooked sweet potatoes, cooked butternut squash, or fresh pumpkin if you don't have any on hand. To get a smooth texture, just make sure the ingredient is boiled, all seeds and skins are removed, and it is thoroughly blended.
- Apple pie spice extract and pumpkin pie spice extract are both options.
- Nutmeg

Adding extra nutmeg is optional. You can therefore omit this ingredient if you don't have any.

DIRECTIONS:

- In a saucepan, mix the egg yolks, corn syrup, and sugar. Mix the items thoroughly using a whisk.
- Add the pumpkin puree, heavy cream, milk, nutmeg, pumpkin pie spice, and extract (optional). Till everything is thoroughly incorporated, stir continuously.
- On a burner, stir the mixture while it is heated to medium. Stir the mixture continuously until an instant-read thermometer reads 165 degrees Fahrenheit.
- Disconnect the stove. As soon as the liquid is off the stove, strain it through a mesh strainer into a pint-sized Ninja Creami container.
- The pint container should be placed in an ice water and ice basin to cool.
- Cover the pint container with the lid and freeze it for 24 hours.
- Take the pint out of the freezer and take the top off after 24 hours.
- Insert a pint into the outside bowl of the Ninja Creami machine.
- Decide on the gelato method.
- Take the pint out of the Ninja Creami after the procedure is finished.
- Dish out and savor!

INGREDIENTS:

- Heavy Cream
  If you don't have heavy cream, you can use butter and milk. Melted 1/4 cup butter and 3/4 cup milk are combined to form 1 cup of heavy cream. Combine well.
- This recipe called for whole milk, which was utilised. Even if milk with a reduced fat level is an option, the final product might not be as rich and creamy.
- Honey is advised, but if you don't have any, you can substitute maple syrup.
- Goat cheese

Goat cheese is now widely available in a variety of flavours at supermarkets. Even goat cheese sweetened with honey is available. Cream cheese can be substituted for goat cheese if you'd prefer.

- Jam

For this dish, raspberry or blackberry jam is suggested. You can substitute another taste if you'd like.

- Lemon curd

You have the option of making your own or purchasing it from a store. Usually, it's close to the jams and jellies.

- Almonds

We used toasted almonds. However, you can substitute cashews, walnuts, or pecans if you'd like.

- Rosemary

Fresh rosemary is ideal because it will give the ice cream a more vibrant flavour. To bring out even more flavour, make sure to toast it before mixing it into the ice cream.

DIRECTIONS:

- In a small pan, mix the cream, milk, and honey; heat to a warm consistency. The mixture must not be allowed to boil.
- Goat cheese should be added to the hot mixture and well mixed after that.
- Fill a pint jar with the mixture, then freeze it for a full day.
- Once the pint container has been frozen for 24 hours, take it out and leave it on the counter for 5 to 10 minutes.
- After placing it in the outer bowl of the Ninja Creami Machine, the pint container of Ninja Creami should be placed there. The ICE CREAM procedure should be chosen.

- When the ICE CREAM procedure is finished, take the pint from the Ninja Creami and poke a 1-inch hole through the centre of the ice cream.
- Cream, milk, and honey should all be combined in a small saucepan. Mixture should be heated until it is hot. Keep the mixture from boiling.
- Once the sauce is warm, stir in the goat cheese and fully combine.
- The mixture should be poured into a Ninja Creami pint container and put in the freezer for 24 hours.
- After 24 hours, take the pint container out of the freezer and let it sit there for five to ten minutes.
- Place the pint container of Ninja Creami into the outside bowl before placing it into the Ninja Creami machine. Select the ICE CREAM approach.

INGREDIENTS:

- Half and Half—Half and Half is a mixture of milk and cream. In essence, you may create your own half-and-half by combining cream and milk. As opposed to measuring out the cream and milk separately, I find that buying half and half is more convenient. Even non-dairy milk is an option.

- Although any milk or non-dairy substitute can be used, whole milk was utilised.

- Make sure to use the INSTANT pudding mix, which is flavor-vanilla. Modified cornstarch is used to make instant pudding mix. This recipe can be made with vanilla, blueberry, or cheesecake flavors. If you're not in the US or don't have access to instant pudding mix, you can come up with a custom substitute.

- There are other recipe variants available online, but the basic method for making INSTANT pudding mix involves mixing 1 part modified cornstarch, such Ez Gel, with 2 parts sugar, followed by flavouring, to the ice cream base. I use 2 tablespoons of INSTANT pudding mix in a lot of my dishes. I would replace it with 2 teaspoons of modified cornstarch, 4 teaspoons of sugar (or a sugar replacement), and a trace quantity of flavour extract. Since this recipe calls for 2 tablespoons of pudding mix, you can replace 2 teaspoons of EZ Gel, 4 teaspoons of sugar or a sugar alternative, and a little quantity of vanilla essence for the 2 teaspoons of pudding mix.

- A comparable item to Instant Pudding that is sold in other nations is called Angel Delight. If all you have is ordinary cornstarch, you might try heating your ice cream base with it, letting it cool, and then putting it in the freezer. Although I haven't tried it, a Facebook user from the Ninja Creami Community suggested it.

- Fresh blueberries were used to create a kind of blueberry compote for this recipe. You may substitute peaches or raspberries or even blackberries for the cranberries, but I wouldn't suggest using frozen fruits because they usually have a lot more moisture when they defrost. The compote will become less delicious and waterier as a result of the extra liquid. However, a pre-made compote or pie filling can be used in place of the blueberries, lemon juice, and some of the sugar. Pie filling in a can often contains a lot of sugar, so use caution when purchasing it.

- Sugar: Any sugar alternative may be used, but I advise using granulated sugar or sugar substitute while creating the crust rather than liquid.
- Although there are many other variations of the recipe available online, INSTANT pudding mix is fundamentally prepared by mixing 1 part modified cornstarch, such as Ez Gel, with 2 parts sugar and then flavouring the ice cream base. 2 tablespoons of INSTANT pudding mix are a common ingredient in my recipes. In its place, I would mix 2 teaspoons of modified cornstarch with 4 teaspoons of sugar, a sugar replacement, and a tiny bit of flavour extract. In place of the 2 tablespoons of pudding mix called for in the recipe, you can add 2 teaspoons of EZ Gel (modified cornstarch), 4 teaspoons of sugar, or a sugar alternative, and a little quantity of vanilla essence.
- Lemon Juice: In general, I advise utilising fresh fruits and vegetables. Using lemon juice from a bottle is perfectly OK in this recipe! It is not necessary to purchase an entire lemon for the recipe because just a tiny amount of lemon juice is required.
- Graham Cracker: Graham crackers are advised, although any crunchy, cinnamon- or vanilla-flavored cookie will do. Teddy Grahams would be excellent!
- Salted butter should be used instead of unsalted. Prior to use, make sure to melt it.
- Nutmeg and allspice are suitable alternatives to cinnamon (ground). You can omit it if none of these alternatives are available to you.

DIRECTIONS:

- Blueberries, sugar, and lemon juice should all be combined in a small pot to make the pie filling. Stir continuously over medium heat until the sugar has dissolved and the blueberries have burst and taken on the consistency of saucy sauce. It should only take a few minutes. While creating the ice cream base, let the mixture cool.

- Put the milk, half-and-half, and pudding mix into the Ninja Creami pint container to make the ice cream base. The whisk should be used to thoroughly combine.
- Combine the ice cream base and the blueberry pie filling in the Ninja Creami Pint container.
- Cover the pint container with its lid and freeze it on a flat place for 24 hours. Take the pint out of the freezer after 24 hours has passed. Take the cover off.
- Take the pint out of the freezer after 24 hours. Remove the lid.
- Insert the Ninja Creami pint into the outer bowl. Turn the Ninja Creami machine while inserting the outer bowl with the pint inside. Press the ICE CREAM button. The ice cream will blend together and acquire a very creamy texture throughout the ice cream function.
- Combine the crust ingredients (making sure the butter is melted) and stir until thoroughly blended.
- After the ice cream function is finished, turn the outer bowl and remove it from the Ninja Creami device.
- Create a hole in the ice cream's middle, then fill it with the crust mixture.
- Refill the Ninja Creami pint there and proceed with the mix-ins.
- It's time to devour your ice cream! Enjoy!

Italian ice, light ice cream, and sorbet are all combined in this dish. Because it is created with fruit, it is sorbet. It is Italian Ice because the basis is lemonade, and it is ice cream because cream cheese and milk are added to give it a slight creamy texture. Italian Ice is less icy than the texture, which is neither as smooth as ice cream. The color and flavour that the blueberries provided to the sorbet are outstanding, even though I only put a small amount of them to the recipe. A few blueberries were quite effective.

To slightly alter the texture, if desired, you can add more milk, cream cheese, or blueberries. More milk and cream cheese will make the mixture creamier and more like ice cream. More blueberries will make the mixture slightly more like sorbet.

INGREDIENTS:

- Lemonade: At the grocery store's cooler area, I purchased pre-made lemonade. For this recipe, you can use any brand of pre-made lemonade. If you care about your health, keep an eye on the sugar content. The final product will be sweeter if there is more sugar in it.
- I used fresh blueberries, but you could also use frozen blueberries in their place. Strawberries, raspberries, or blackberries can be used in place of blueberries. Although the texture of the sorbet will alter because these other berries typically contain more seeds.
- Reduced-fat or full-fat cream cheese will work. Add an extra 1–2 tablespoons of cream cheese for a creamier and less frosty texture at the very end.
- Any milk would work; I used full milk. The texture won't be the same as using regular milk if you use non-dairy milk, so keep that in mind. The texture of non-dairy milk is frequently icier. Instead of utilizing the SORBET function when using non-dairy milk, utilize the LITE ICE CREAM function.

DIRECTIONS:

- In a medium mixing bowl, whisk the milk and softened cream cheese together. Attempt to blend the two as much as you can. There may still be a few little cream cheese bits, but that's okay as long as they are tiny.
- Include the lemonade and well combine.
- Transfer the mixture to a Ninja Creami pint container, top with the blueberries, and freeze for a full 24 hours on a level surface in a cold freezer.
- Take the pint out of the freezer after 24 hours. Take off the lid.
- In the outer bowl, put the pint of Ninja Creami. Turn the Ninja Creami machine while inserting the outer bowl with the pint. The outer bowl should lock into place. Sorbet the button. The sorbet will combine and get quite creamy during the SORBET action. It ought should take around two minutes.
- After the SORBET function is finished, turn the outer bowl and unplug the Ninja Creami device.
- You can now taste your sorbet! Enjoy!

If the sorbet isn't quite creamy enough, re-insert the pint-sized outer bowl into the Ninja Creami machine and lock it in place. Select RE-SPIN as your function. Remove the outer bowl from the Ninja Creami when it has finished its RE-SPIN cycle.

NINJA CREAMI BLUEBERRY-RASPBERRY ICE-CREAM

INGREDIENTS:

- Half and Half—Half and Half is a mixture of milk and cream. In essence, you may create your own half-and-half by combining cream and milk. As opposed to measuring out the cream and milk separately, I find that buying half and half is more convenient. Even non-dairy milk is an option.
- Although any milk or non-dairy substitute can be used, whole milk was utilised.
- Make sure to use the INSTANT pudding mix, which is flavor-vanilla. Modified cornstarch is used to make instant pudding mix. This recipe can be made with vanilla, blueberry, or cheesecake flavors. If you're not in the US or don't have access to instant pudding mix, you can come up with a custom substitute.
- There are other recipe variants available online, but the basic method for making INSTANT pudding mix involves mixing 1 part modified cornstarch, such Ez Gel, with 2 parts sugar, followed by flavouring, to the ice cream base. I use 2 tablespoons of INSTANT pudding mix in a lot of my dishes. I would replace it with 2 teaspoons of modified cornstarch, 4 teaspoons of sugar (or a sugar replacement), and a trace quantity of flavour extract. Since this recipe calls for 2 tablespoons of pudding mix, you can replace 2 teaspoons of EZ Gel, 4 teaspoons of sugar or a sugar alternative, and a little quantity of vanilla essence for the 2 teaspoons of pudding mix.
- A comparable item to Instant Pudding that is sold in other nations is called Angel Delight. If all you have is ordinary cornstarch, you might try heating your ice cream base with it, letting it cool, and then putting it in the freezer. Although I haven't tried it, a Facebook user from the Ninja Creami Community suggested it.
- Fresh blueberries and raspberries were used to create a kind of blueberry raspberry compote for this recipe. You may substitute peaches or raspberries or even blackberries for the cranberries, but I wouldn't suggest using frozen fruits because they usually have a lot

more moisture when they defrost. The compote will become less delicious and waterier as a result of the extra liquid. However, a pre-made compote or pie filling can be used in place of the blueberries, lemon juice, and some of the sugar. Pie filling in a can often contains a lot of sugar, so use caution when purchasing it.

- Sugar: Any sugar alternative may be used, but I advise using granulated sugar or sugar substitute while creating the crust rather than liquid.
- Although there are many other variations of the recipe available online, INSTANT pudding mix is fundamentally prepared by mixing 1 part modified cornstarch, such as Ez Gel, with 2 parts sugar and then flavouring the ice cream base. 2 tablespoons of INSTANT pudding mix are a common ingredient in my recipes. In its place, I would mix 2 teaspoons of modified cornstarch with 4 teaspoons of sugar, a sugar replacement, and a tiny bit of flavour extract. In place of the 2 tablespoons of pudding mix called for in the recipe, you can add 2 teaspoons of EZ Gel (modified cornstarch), 4 teaspoons of sugar, or a sugar alternative, and a little quantity of vanilla essence.
- Lemon Juice: In general, I advise utilizing fresh fruits and vegetables. Using lemon juice from a bottle is perfectly OK in this recipe! It is not necessary to purchase an entire lemon for the recipe because just a tiny amount of lemon juice is required.
- Graham Cracker: Graham crackers are advised, although any crunchy, cinnamon- or vanilla-flavored cookie will do. Teddy Grahams would be excellent!
- Salted butter should be used instead of unsalted. Prior to use, make sure to melt it.
- Nutmeg and allspice are suitable alternatives to cinnamon (ground). You can omit it if none of these alternatives are available to you.

DIRECTIONS:

- Blueberries, Raspberries sugar, and lemon juice should all be combined in a small pot to make the pie filling. Stir continuously over medium heat until the sugar has dissolved and the blueberries have burst and taken on the consistency of saucy sauce. It should only take a few minutes. While creating the ice cream base, let the mixture cool.

- Put the milk, half-and-half, and pudding mix into the Ninja Creami pint container to make the ice cream base. The whisk should be used to thoroughly combine.
- Combine the ice cream base and the blueberry pie filling in the Ninja Creami Pint container.
- Cover the pint container with its lid and freeze it on a flat place for 24 hours. Take the pint out of the freezer after 24 hours has passed. Take the cover off.
- Take the pint out of the freezer after 24 hours. Remove the lid.
- Insert the Ninja Creami pint into the outer bowl. Turn the Ninja Creami machine while inserting the outer bowl with the pint inside. Press the ICE CREAM button. The ice cream will blend together and acquire a very creamy texture throughout the ice cream function.
- Combine the crust ingredients (making sure the butter is melted) and stir until thoroughly blended.
- After the ice cream function is finished, turn the outer bowl and remove it from the Ninja Creami device.
- Create a hole in the ice cream's middle, then fill it with the crust mixture.
- Refill the Ninja Creami pint there and proceed with the mix-ins.
- It's time to devour your ice cream! Enjoy!

There is no need to search any farther if you want a tasty and healthful dessert. You can completely control what you eat and make mango sorbet with the Ninja Creami in a matter of minutes. You can even use fresh mangoes if you'd like, and this mango sorbet has no strange or difficult-to-pronounce ingredients. It couldn't be simpler to make mango sorbet with the Ninja Creami. The hardest part, in all honesty, is waiting the whole 24 hours for it to freeze before creamifying it. The tinned mango is transformed into a super-creamy sorbet with a mango flavour after being creamified. The texture is incredibly creamy, which is truly great. This recipe doesn't contain any extra flavours or colors. Additionally, making it is quite simple.

INGREDIENTS:

MANGO

I used a 15-ounce can of sliced mangoes in extra-light syrup for the mango. Mangoes can be used fresh or in canned form, chopped or sliced. Mangoes are sold diced and sold in light or heavy syrup. For this dish, any will work. Just purchase the amount of sweetness that you find most appealing.

DIRECTIONS:

- I used a 15-ounce can of sliced mangoes in extra-light syrup for the mango. Mangoes can be used fresh or in canned form, chopped or sliced. Mangoes are sold diced and sold in light or heavy syrup. For this dish, any will work. Just purchase the amount of sweetness that you find most appealing.

NINJA CREAMI FRUIT PARADISE SORBET

INGREDIENTS:

- You can use any canned fruit in place of pineapple, even pineapple.
- You can replace your preferred canned fruit for the grapefruit in this dish.
- You can replace your preferred canned fruit with the mandarin oranges.
- The bananas utilised were brand-new ones. The use of frozen bananas is not advised because the bananas will be crushed and combined with the other components.
- If preferred, you can skip the maraschino cherries in jars.

DIRECTIONS:

- Fill the big bowl with the fruit, juice included.
- Bananas are added to the fruit dish after being peeled and sliced.
- Incorporate the fruit with the bananas.
- Fourth, thoroughly combine.
- 5. Fill to the top of a pint container and secure the lid. You'll have enough remaining to create three pints (see below for an optional idea.)
- Let the food remain frozen for a day.
- Take the pint out of the freezer after 24 hours has passed. In the outer dish, place the pint after removing the cover. Put the outer bowl in, then select the "Sorbet" option.
- Remove the pint and serve after the Ninja Creami's sorbet function is complete.
- Optional: After the sorbet has finished processing, remove the pint and use a spoon to create a well in the middle of the dessert. Maraschino cherries should be added, then turn on Mix-Ins.
- The remaining mixture can be poured into a deep baking pan and frozen if you don't have enough pint containers to freeze the entire batch. To serve, let food defrost a little before removing it from the baking pan.

NINJA CREAMI LEMON PEACH ICE-CREAM WITH WHISKY

INGREDIENTS:

- Fair life Whole Milk, 1 3/4 cups
- Jell-O Lemon Flavor Instant Pudding, three tablespoons
- Torani Peach Syrup, 1 tablespoon
- 1 Tablespoon of whiskey with a Georgia peach flavour

DIRECTIONS:

- Fill a Ninja Creami pint with everything.
- Stir for two minutes with whisk.
- For 24 hours, place the covered container in the freezer on a flat surface.
- Take out of the freezer after 24 hours.
- Put the pint container in the machine's outer bowl after doing so.
- Select "Gelato" as the function and procedure.
- Enjoy your meal after you've prepared it.

A "cobbler"-like mix-ins can be made in countless different ways. However, because I prefer to keep things simple, I used "honey bunches of oats, simply the bunches." If you're looking for something straightforward, just the bunches are the way to go. If you want, you can also incorporate robust granola or create your own "cobbler" mix-in. If you substitute something different because the bunches have sugar added, the processed product might not be as sweet. You can just add the bunches to your preferred cereal if you have leftovers.

INGREDIENTS:

- 15.5 ounces of peaches and 12 ounces of peach yoghurt (Noosa, with the fruit on the bottom) (Canned- Slices in heavy syrup- Drain almost all of the syrup)
- 1 teaspoon sugar, 1/2 teaspoon vanilla bean paste, or vanilla extract (White or brown)
- A 1/4 teaspoon of cinnamon (Ground)
- 14 cup honey-bunches-just the bundles of oats
- One teaspoon milk

DIRECTIONS:

- In a Ninja Creami Pint, combine the yoghurt, sugar, cinnamon, vanilla bean paste, and half of the peaches (without the syrup). Mix thoroughly by stirring. For a full 24 hours, place a level surface in a cold freezer and freeze.
- Take the pint out of the freezer after 24 hours has passed. Take the cover off.
- In the outer bowl, put the pint of Ninja Creami. Turn the Ninja Creami machine while inserting the outer bowl with the pint. The outer bowl should lock into place. Activate the LITE ICE CREAM button. The yoghurt will blend together and become creamy during the LITE ICE CREAM function. It ought should take around two minutes.

- If the frozen yoghurt is brittle and dry, don't become alarmed. Create a hole in the frozen yogurt's middle, then add the leftover peaches (without the syrup) and Honey Bunches of Oats. If it's dry and crumbly, add a teaspoon of milk.
- Reintroduce the Ninja Creami pint to the outer bowl. Turn the Ninja Creami machine while inserting the outer bowl with the pint. The outer bowl should lock into place. Press the "MIX INS" button to begin.
- It's time to enjoy your frozen yoghurt! Enjoy!

NINJA CREAMI VANILLA YOGHURT ICREAM

INGREDIENTS:

- 16-ounces vanilla yoghurt

DIRECTIONS:

- Place 16 ounces of yoghurt in a Ninja Creami pint container, level it out, and freeze for a full 24 hours in a cold freezer.
- Take the pint out of the freezer after 24 hours has passed. Take the cover off.
- In the outer bowl, put the pint of Ninja Creami. Turn the Ninja Creami machine while inserting the outer bowl with the pint. The outer bowl should lock into place. Activate the LITE ICE CREAM button. The yoghurt will blend together and become creamy during the LITE ICE CREAM function. It ought should take around two minutes.
- After the LITE ICE CREAM feature has finished, spin the outer bowl and remove it from the Ninja Creami device.
- You can now eat your frozen yoghurt. Enjoy!

NINJA CREAMI HOT CINNAMON SPICE FROZEN YOGHURT ICE-CREAM

INGREDIENTS:

- 1 cup of Harney & Sons
- Hot Cinnamon Spice Tea,
- 1/2 cup of nonfat Greek yoghurt,
- 1 teaspoon of sugar-free Torani Vanilla syrup,
- and 1/8 cup of allulose

DIRECTIONS:

- In a Creami pint container, combine each item.
- Insert into the machine after adding a pint container to the outside bowl.
- To combine ingredients, spin the blender using the "milkshake" option.
- From the outer bowl, take out pint.
- 24 hours of freezing.
- Take the pint out of the freezer after 24 hours has passed.
- Insert into the machine after adding a pint container to the outside bowl.
- A "Lite ice cream" setting should be selected.
- If you don't like the texture and consistency, respin the food once or twice.
- Enjoy your food!

NINJA CREAMI PEANUT BUTTER BANANA ICE-CREAM

INGREDIENTS:

- 4-5 Ripe Bananas, cut into chunks of 1-2 inches (more or less, depending on the size of the bananas). I used tiny bananas; you might only need 2 or 3 if you're using very huge bananas.)
- 1/2 cup of peanut butter
- 1/4 cup of dark cocoa powder
- 1/4 cup of half-and-half mix-ins
- 1/4 cup of chocolate chunks (or Chips)

DIRECTIONS:

- Blend the following ingredients in a blender: bananas, peanut butter, chocolate powder, and half and half.
- Pour everything into a Ninja Creami Pint bottle.
- The pint container's lid should be on, and it should be frozen for 24 hours on a level surface. Take the pint out of the freezer after 24 hours has passed. Take the cover off.
- Take the pint out of the freezer after 24 hours has passed. Take the cover off.
- In the outer bowl, put the pint of Ninja Creami. Turn the Ninja Creami machine while inserting the outer bowl with the pint. The outer bowl should lock into place. Make use of the ICE CREAM button. The ice cream will blend together and get incredibly creamy throughout the ice cream function.
- In a Creami pint container, combine each item.
- Insert into the machine after adding a pint container to the outside bowl.
- To combine ingredients, spin the blender using the "milkshake" option.
- From the outer bowl, take out pint.
- 24 hours of freezing.
- Take the pint out of the freezer after 24 hours has passed.
- Insert into the machine after adding a pint container to the outside bowl.

- A "Lite ice cream" setting should be selected.
- If you don't like the texture and consistency, re-spin the food once or twice.
- Enjoy your food

NINJA CREAMI STRAWBERRY ICE-CREAM

INGREDIENTS:

- Oatmeal in (case you are not having cream)
- Milk (any) ALMOND would make it awesome
- Cream
- Strawberries
- Chunks
- Sprinkles

DIRECTIONS:

- The next thing you are supposed to do is to freeze cream/oatmeal/ strawberries together in a freezer for at least 24 hours. Put it in the Creami after chilling it for the night and spun it on ice-cream. You will feel some crumbliness in your ice-cream, and it will turn out so flakier just like Dippin' Dots. It will almost icier (similar to Halo Top and those other light ice creams). While it didn't turn out looking like typical and ordinary ice cream, it tasted fairly good. So better results mixed them with some Reese's Pieces and chunks than ran it through the mixer. If then serving, serve with some sprinkles and chunks that will increase more it's taste and this will be going to be the delicious easy prep strawberry ice-cream at home with Ninja. Must add strawberry pieces before serving.

NINJA CREAMI LEMON COOKIE ICE-CREAM

INGREDIENTS:

- Lemon extract
- Cream Cheese
- Chocolate chips
- Golden Oreos

DIRECTIONS:

- Blend the following ingredients in a blender: lemon extract, Cream cheese, chocolate powder, and some oreos.Pour everything into a Ninja Creami Pint bottle.
- The pint container's lid should be on, and it should be frozen for 24 hours on a level surface. Take the pint out of the freezer after 24 hours has passed. Take the cover off.
- Take the pint out of the freezer after 24 hours has passed. Take the cover off.
- In the outer bowl, put the pint of Ninja Creami. Turn the Ninja Creami machine while inserting the outer bowl with the pint. The outer bowl should lock into place. Make use of the ICE CREAM button. The ice cream will blend together and get incredibly creamy throughout the ice cream function.In a Creami pint container, combine each item.
- Insert into the machine after adding a pint container to the outside bowl.
- To combine ingredients, spin the blender using the "milkshake" option.
- From the outer bowl, take out pint.
- 24 hours of freezing.
- Take the pint out of the freezer after 24 hours has passed.
- Insert into the machine after adding a pint container to the outside bowl.
- A "Lite ice cream" setting should be selected.
- If you don't like the texture and consistency, re-spin the food once or twice.
- Enjoy your food

INGREDIENTS:

- Milk
- sugar
- Cream Cheese
- Chocolate chips
- egg

DIRECTIONS:

- In a pint-sized Ninja Creami container that is empty, pour eggnog. For 24 hours, place the cover on and freeze.
- Take the pint out of the freezer 24 hours after freezing it. Take the cover off.
- Insert the pint into the outer basin. Turn the Ninja Creami machine while inserting the outer bowl with the pint. The outer bowl should lock into place. By pressing the GELATO button. The ice cream will combine and thicken up during the gelato process.
- After the GELATO function is finished, rotate the outer bowl and remove it from the Ninja Creami device. Make a hole along the middle, add a spoonful of eggnog or milk, and then re-spin the eggnog if it is crumbly or dry.
- If your machine doesn't have a gelato setting, you can still produce Ninja Creami Eggnog Ice Cream by processing ice cream. Even while it might not be quite as thick and creamy, the outcome will still be fantastic.)
- It's time to taste your ice cream! Enjoy

NINJA CREAMI PISTACHIO ICE-CREAM

INGREDIENTS:

- Oatmeal in (case you are not having cream)
- Milk (any) ALMOND would make it awesome
- Cream
- Pistachio
- Chunks
- Sprinkles

DIRECTIONS:

- The next thing you are supposed to do is to freeze cream/oatmeal/ pistachio together in a freezer for at least 24 hours. Put it in the Creami after chilling it for the night and spun it on ice-cream. You will feel some crumbliness in your ice-cream, and it will turn out so flakier just like Dippin' Dots. It will almost icier (similar to Halo Top and those other light ice creams). While it didn't turn out looking like typical and ordinary ice cream, it tasted fairly good. So better results mixed them with some Reese's Pieces and chunks than ran it through the mixer. If then serving, serve with some sprinkles and chunks that will increase more it's taste and this will be going to be the delicious easy prep pistachio ice-cream at home with Ninja. Must add pistachio, chocolate chips toppings pieces before serving.

INGREDIENTS:

- Oatmeal in (case you are not having cream)
- Milk (any) ALMOND would make it awesome
- Cream
- Pistachio
- Chunks
- butter
- Sprinkles

DIRECTIONS:

- We created pistachio gelato that is just as nice as that found in specialty shops. The almond and coconut creamer I use has 10 calories per tablespoon. A cup of that has 160 calories. Also no carbs for people on a ketogenic diet. No lactose. ticks every box in my home. Contrast that with the 50 calories per tablespoon and 800 calories per cup of heavy whipping cream. But the flavour, which is creamy wonderful, is the greatest part. Nothing was given up.
- I processed 1/3 cup of pistachios in a food processor with a tiny bit of oil until the mixture had the consistency of peanut butter. Although it takes longer than you expect, it is worthwhile.
- 1/4 cup monk fruit; choose the type and quantity of sweetener according to your preferences.
- two tablespoons of sugar-free pistachio pudding
- Fill the container to the fill line with nut pod almond and coconut.
- can include additives like chocolate chips or pistachios.
- No re-spin was necessary.
- This is something I could eat daily.

NINJA CREAMI COCONUT ICE-CREAM

INGREDIENTS:

- Oatmeal in (case you are not having cream)
- Milk (any) ALMOND would make it awesome
- Cream
- Coconut
- Coconut powder
- Protein powder
- Chunks
- butter
- Sprinkles of coconut

DIRECTIONS:

- Whoever enjoys coconut ice cream as much as I do.
- Protein powder with the flavour vanilla from PE Science. (Among the best-tasting vanillas I've discovered),
- a small bag of coconut chips,
- Unsweetened coconut milk from Silk, 12 ounces
- 2T sugar-free The Torani Coconut
- Perfect Ice Cream stabilizer, 1/4 teaspoon.
- The taste and smoothness are outstanding despite being so straightforward and sugar-free.
- 1-2 Vootman's sugar-free coconut biscuits are a wonderful add-in.
- Enjoy
  OR
- The next thing you are supposed to do is to freeze cream/oatmeal/ coconut together in a freezer for at least 24 hours. Put it in the Creami after chilling it for the night and spun it on ice-cream. You will feel some crumbliness in your ice-cream, and it will turn out so flakier just like Dippin' Dots. It will almost icier (similar to Halo Top and those other light ice creams). While it didn't turn out looking like typical and ordinary ice cream, it tasted fairly good. So better results mixed them with some Reese's Pieces and chunks than ran it through the mixer. If

then serving, serve with some sprinkles and chunks that will increase more it's taste and this will be going to be the delicious easy prep pistachio ice-cream at home with Ninja. Must add coconut chips, chocolate chips toppings pieces before serving.

NINJA CREAMI FROZEN COFFEE ICE-CREAM

INGREDIENTS:

- Coffee
- Milk
- Coffee chips
- Chocolate chips
- Almond milk
- Chocolate cherry coffee
- K-pod sugar
- cream

DIRECTIONS:

- The next thing you are supposed to do is to freeze cream/oatmeal/ coffee together in a freezer for at least 24 hours. Put it in the Creami after chilling it for the night and spun it on ice-cream. You will feel some crumbliness in your ice-cream, and it will turn out so flakier just like Dippin' Dots. It will almost icier (similar to Halo Top and those other light ice creams). While it didn't turn out looking like typical and ordinary ice cream, it tasted fairly good. So better results mixed them with some Reese's Pieces and chunks than ran it through the mixer. If then serving, serve with some sprinkles and chunks that will increase more it's taste and this will be going to be the delicious easy prep frozen coffee ice-cream at home with Ninja. Must add coffee chips, chocolate chips toppings pieces before serving.

NINJA CREAMI VANILLA-CHOCOLATE ICE-CREAM

INGREDIENTS:

- Half and Half—Half and Half is a mixture of milk and cream. In essence, you may create your own half-and-half by combining cream and milk. As opposed to measuring out the cream and milk separately, I find that buying half and half is more convenient. Even non-dairy milk is an option.
- Although any milk or non-dairy substitute can be used, whole milk was utilised.
- Make sure to use the INSTANT pudding mix, which is flavor-vanilla. Modified cornstarch is used to make instant pudding mix. This recipe can be made with vanilla, blueberry, or cheesecake flavors. If you're not in the US or don't have access to instant pudding mix, you can come up with a custom substitute.
- There are other recipe variants available online, but the basic method for making INSTANT pudding mix involves mixing 1 part modified cornstarch, such Ez Gel, with 2 parts sugar, followed by flavouring, to the ice cream base. I use 2 tablespoons of INSTANT pudding mix in a lot of my dishes. I would replace it with 2 teaspoons of modified cornstarch, 4 teaspoons of sugar (or a sugar replacement), and a trace quantity of flavour extract. Since this recipe calls for 2 tablespoons of pudding mix, you can replace 2 teaspoons of EZ Gel, 4 teaspoons of sugar or a sugar alternative, and a little quantity of vanilla essence for the 2 teaspoons of pudding mix.
- A comparable item to Instant Pudding that is sold in other nations is called Angel Delight. If all you have is ordinary cornstarch, you might try heating your ice cream base with it, letting it cool, and then putting it in the freezer. Although I haven't tried it, a Facebook user from the Ninja Creami Community suggested it.
- Sugar: Any sugar alternative may be used, but I advise using granulated sugar or sugar substitute while creating the crust rather than liquid.

- Although there are many other variations of the recipe available online, INSTANT pudding mix is fundamentally prepared by mixing 1 part modified cornstarch, such as Ez Gel, with 2 parts sugar and then flavouring the ice cream base. 2 tablespoons of INSTANT pudding mix are a common ingredient in my recipes. In its place, I would mix 2 teaspoons of modified cornstarch with 4 teaspoons of sugar, a sugar replacement, and a tiny bit of flavour extract. In place of the 2 tablespoons of pudding mix called for in the recipe, you can add 2 teaspoons of EZ Gel (modified cornstarch), 4 teaspoons of sugar, or a sugar alternative, and a little quantity of vanilla essence.
- Lemon Juice: In general, I advise utilizing fresh fruits and vegetables. Using lemon juice from a bottle is perfectly OK in this recipe! It is not necessary to purchase an entire lemon for the recipe because just a tiny amount of lemon juice is required.
- Graham Cracker: Graham crackers are advised, although any crunchy, cinnamon- or vanilla-flavored cookie will do. Teddy Grahams would be excellent!
- Salted butter should be used instead of unsalted. Prior to use, make sure to melt it.
- Nutmeg and allspice are suitable alternatives to cinnamon (ground). You can omit it if none of these alternatives are available to you.

DIRECTIONS:

- Chocolate, Vanilla, sugar, and lemon juice should all be combined in a small pot to make the pie filling. Stir continuously over medium heat until the sugar has dissolved and the vanilla essence have burst and taken on the consistency of saucy sauce. It should only take a few minutes. While creating the ice cream base, let the mixture cool.
- Put the milk, half-and-half, and pudding mix into the Ninja Creami pint container to make the ice cream base. The whisk should be used to thoroughly combine.
- Combine the ice cream base and the blueberry pie filling in the Ninja Creami Pint container.

- Cover the pint container with its lid and freeze it on a flat place for 24 hours. Take the pint out of the freezer after 24 hours has passed. Take the cover off.
- Take the pint out of the freezer after 24 hours. Remove the lid.
- Insert the Ninja Creami pint into the outer bowl. Turn the Ninja Creami machine while inserting the outer bowl with the pint inside. Press the ICE CREAM button. The ice cream will blend together and acquire a very creamy texture throughout the ice cream function.
- Combine the crust ingredients (making sure the butter is melted) and stir until thoroughly blended.
- After the ice cream function is finished, turn the outer bowl and remove it from the Ninja Creami device.
- Create a hole in the ice cream's middle, then fill it with the crust mixture.
- Refill the Ninja Creami pint there and proceed with the mix-ins.
- It's time to devour your ice cream! Enjoy!

INGREDIENTS:

- Pumpkin Spice Greek Yogurt
- 1 Atkins Creamy Cinnamon Swirl Protein Shake, and 1 tablespoon Jell-O Cheesecake pudding powder
- 1 teaspoon pumpkin spice (or 1/4 teaspoon if using pumpkin protein smoothie)

DIRECTIONS:

- Freeze for 24 hours, microwave for 30 seconds
- level the top, blend using the smoothie bowl setting
- scrape down the sides, add a little extra protein shake
- and then spin again to serve.
- I topped it with some pumpkin whipped topping and high-key ginger spice cookies.
- Enjoy your ice-cream with Ninja.

NINJA CREAMI EASY S'MORES ICE-CREAM

INGREDIENTS:

- 8 substantial marshmallows
- a half-cup of whole milk
- 3/4 cup of heavy cream
- a tsp. of sea salt
- 1/3 cup sugar crystals
- 1 softened spoonful of cream cheese
- Topping of a pinch of sea salt and 1/4 cup of micro dark chocolate chips, along with 1/2 cup of broken graham crackers

DIRECTIONS:

- A baking sheet should be foil-lined. Place the marshmallows on the baking sheet and broil for 5 to 7 minutes, or until they are browned. After cooling, take the marshmallows out of the oven.
- Cream cheese should be heated for 20 seconds in a sizable microwave-safe bowl. With a whisk or rubber spatula, combine the sugar and sea salt and continue mixing for approximately a minute, or until the mixture resembles frosting.
- Heavy cream and milk should be gradually incorporated after the sugar has been dissolved.
- Add the cooled marshmallows to the base and blend after they have cooled. An empty CREAMi should be filled with base. Put the pint's storage lid on, then freeze it for a day.
- Take the pint out of the freezer and take the lid off. Put a pint in the outer bowl, attach the CREAMi Paddle to the lid of the outer bowl, and secure the lid assembly. Place the bowl assembly on the motor base, then elevate the platform and lock it in place by turning the handle to the right.
- Choose ICE CREAM.
- Make a hole with a spoon that is 1 12 inches wide and reaches the pint's bottom. Then, using the MIX-IN software, add the dark chocolate chips and graham cracker crumbs to the hole.

- Remove the ice cream from the pint after processing is finished, sprinkle a pint of sea salt on top, and serve right away.

NINJA CREAMI SPIKED SELTZER SHERBET ICE-CREAM

INGREDIENTS:

- 1 1/2 cups of rainbow sherbet from the store
- Truly Lime Seltzer in a half-cup

DIRECTIONS:

- In the sequence specified, add each ingredient to a CREAMi Pint that is empty.
- Put a pint in the outer bowl, attach the Creamerizer paddle to the lid of the outer bowl, and secure the lid assembly to the outer bowl. Place the bowl assembly on the motor base, then lift the platform by turning the handle to the right and locking it in place.
- Select on MILKSHAKE.
- After processing is finished, remove the milkshake from the pint and serve right away.

NINJA CREAMI SPIKED SELTZER SHERBET SHAKE

INGREDIENTS:

- 1 1/2 cups of rainbow sherbet from the store
- Truly Lime Seltzer in a half-cup

DIRECTIONS:

- In the sequence specified, add each ingredient to a CREAMi Pint that is empty.
- Put a pint in the outer bowl, attach the Creamerizer paddle to the lid of the outer bowl, and secure the lid assembly to the outer bowl. Place the bowl assembly on the motor base, then lift the platform by turning the handle to the right and locking it in place.
- Select on MILKSHAKE.
- After processing is finished, remove the milkshake from the pint and serve right away.

NINJA CREAMI ORANGE SHERBET

INGREDIENTS:

- 1 1/2 cups of rainbow sherbet from the store
- Orange juice in a half-cup
- Orange pulp for the pulp lovers

DIRECTIONS:

- In the sequence specified, add each ingredient to a CREAMi Pint that is empty.
- Put a pint in the outer bowl, attach the Creamerizer paddle to the lid of the outer bowl, and secure the lid assembly to the outer bowl. Place the bowl assembly on the motor base, then lift the platform by turning the handle to the right and locking it in place.
- Select on MILKSHAKE.
- After processing is finished, remove the milkshake from the pint and serve right away.

INGREDIENTS:

- 4 big yolks of eggs
- 1 teaspoon sugar substitute for corn
- 1 tablespoon plus 1/4 cup of granulated sugar
- heavy cream, 1 cup
- 1 cup of whole milk
- 1 tsp. of peppermint oil
- 1/4 cup crushed candy canes or peppermints

DIRECTIONS:

- Whisk together the egg yolks, corn syrup, and sugar in a small saucepan until the sugar has completely dissolved.
- Stir together the milk, peppermint extract, and heavy cream in the pot.
- While whisking continuously, place the saucepan on the stovetop at medium heat. On an instant-read thermometer, cook until the internal temperature reaches 170F.
- After removing it from the stove, pour the base into a CREAMi Pint that has not yet been filled. In an ice bath, put a pint. Place the pint's storage cover on it after it has cooled, then freeze it for 24 hours.
- Remove the pint's lid and take it out of the freezer. Put a pint of liquid in the outer bowl, attach the lid assembly to the outer bowl, and lock it in place. Place the bowl assembly on the motor base, then lift the platform by turning the handle to the right and locking it in place.
- Choose GELATO.
- Make a hole that is 1 12 inches broad and reaches the pint's bottom with a spoon. Use the MIX-IN software to process the pint one more after adding crushed peppermint or candy cane bits.
- Once processing is finished, remove the gelato from the pint and serve right away.

NINJA CREAMI MULLED APPLE CIDER ICE-CREAM

INGREDIENTS:

- heavy cream, 1 cup
- 50 ml of whole milk
- Mott's®, half a cup apple juice
- Vanilla extract, 1 teaspoon
- a third cup of light brown sugar
- divided into 1 teaspoon and 1/4 teaspoon of ground cinnamon
- pinch of nutmeg, ground
- pinch of allspice, ground
- little amount of ground cloves
- Orange zest, 2 tablespoons
- 1/8 cup butter for topping
- Topping: 1/2 cup chopped, peeled, and cored Granny Smith apples

DIRECTIONS:

- Mix the cream, whole milk, Mott's® Apple Cider, vanilla extract, brown sugar, 1/2 teaspoon cinnamon, 1/4 teaspoon each of ground nutmeg, ground cloves, and ground allspice in a large basin until well blended.
- Fill a CREAMi container with base. Put a storage lid on the pint, then freeze it for a day.
- Put the butter in a small pot and warm it up on the stovetop to make the apple topping. Add the apples and remaining cinnamon once the icecream.

INGREDIENTS:

- 2 cups of frozen chunks of pitaya (dragon fruit)
- 12,000 ml of pineapple juice
- TOPPINGS (OPTIONAL)
- Sliced bananas
- Mixed berries
- A seed or nut

DIRECTIONS:

- Pitaya bits should be added to a CREAMI Pint until it reaches the MAX FILL line.
- Next, pour enough pineapple juice to completely saturate the pitaya. There won't be a need for two complete cans of pineapple juice. Pitaya and pineapple juice should be mixed, and extra juice can be added if necessary to fill the container to the top. Put the pint's storage lid on, then freeze it for a day.
- Remove the pint's lid and take it out of the freezer. Put a pint in the outer bowl, attach the CREAMi Paddle to the lid, and secure the lid assembly to the outer bowl. Place the bowl assembly on the motor base, then lift the platform by turning the handle to the right and locking it in place.
- Opt for SMOOTHIE BOWL.
- Transfer to a bowl once the processing is finished, then top with your preferred garnishes.

NINJA CREAMI TRULY SANGRIA SORBET

INGREDIENTS:

- TRULY Holiday Sangria Seltzer, 1/2 cup
- A raw agave nectar in three tablespoons
- 1 can (15 1/4 ounces) of heavy syrup-covered tropical fruit, drained, without the syrup.

DIRECTIONS:

- Agave must be well dissolved before adding it to the seltzer.
- Tropical fruit should be added until the MAX FILL line in a CREAMi Pint that is empty. Until the MAX FILL line is reached, add seltzer and agave mixture to peaches. Pint should be covered with a storage lid and frozen for a day.
- After removing the pint's cover, take it out of the freezer. Put a pint of liquid inside the outer bowl, attach the Creamerizer paddle to the lid, and secure the lid assembly to the outside bowl. To raise the platform and secure it in position, set the bowl assembly on the motor base and twist the handle to the right.
- Choose SORBET
- Remove the sorbet from the pint and serve it right away after processing is finished

NINJA CREAMI WATERMELON MINT SORBET FLOAT

INGREDIENTS:

- diced 3 cups of fresh watermelon
- 1/3 cup sugar crystals
- Juice of two teaspoons of lemon
- ten new leaves of mint
- A half-cup of REAL Watermelon Lemonade Hard Seltzer and any further reserves

DIRECTIONS:

- In a blender, combine all the ingredients, and blend on HIGH for about a minute, or until smooth.
- Fill a CREAMi pint all the way to the MAX FILL line with liquid. Put a storage lid on the pint, then freeze it for a day.
- Take the pint out of the freezer and take the lid off. Put a pint of liquid in the outer bowl, attach the Creamerizer Paddle to the lid of the outer bowl, and secure the lid assembly to the outer bowl. Place the bowl assembly on the motor base, then elevate the platform and lock it in place by turning the handle to the right.
- Choose SORBET.
- Add a scoop of sorbet on top. Mint is a nice garnish, and serve right away.

NINJA CREAMI MAPLE GELATO

For this all you need is this

COOKING TIME:10-minutes

INGREDIENTS:

- 4 big yolks of eggs
- maple syrup, 1 tbsp
- 1 tablespoon plus half a cup of light brown sugar
- 1 teaspoon maple flavouring (optional)
- 30 ml of thick cream
- 1 glass of whole milk

DIRECTIONS:

- A small pot should be used to mix and dissolve the sugar after adding the egg yolks, maple syrup, sugar, and maple essence.
- Stir together the heavy cream and milk in the pot.
- Put a saucepan on the burner and whisk continuously with a rubber spatula. Cook until an instant-read thermometer reads between 165 and 175 degrees Fahrenheit.
- After removing it from the heat, pour the foundation into a CREAMi that has not yet been filled. In an ice bath, put a pint. Place storage cover on pint after it has cooled, then freeze for 24 hours.
- Take the pint out of the freezer and take the lid off. Put a pint of liquid in the outer bowl, attach the Creamerizer Paddle to the lid of the outer bowl, and secure the lid assembly to the outer bowl. Place the bowl assembly on the motor base, then elevate the platform and lock it in place by turning the handle to the right.
- Pick GELATO.
- Add mix-ins or remove the gelato from the pint and serve right away after processing is finished.

INGREDIENTS:

- 1/9 cup cream cheese
- Unsweetened cocoa powder, 2 tablespoons
- One teaspoon of vanilla extract and Granulated Sugar, 1/3 cup
- Milk, whole, 1 cup and 3/4 cups Cream Heavy
- 1/8 teaspoon of cinnamon, ground
- 1/fourth teaspoon of chilli powder

DIRECTIONS:

- 1 tablespoon of cream cheese should be microwaved for 5 to 10 seconds in a medium bowl. The five to ten seconds in the microwave will assist soften cream cheese if it was in the fridge so that it can combine properly with the other components.1 teaspoon vanilla extract, 3 cups of sugar, and 2 tablespoons of unsweetened cocoa powder should all be combined with cream cheese. Mix the ingredients together by whisking.
- Stir in 1/4 teaspoon each of cinnamon powder and chilli powder. If you want more heat, swap out 1/4 tsp of the chilli powder for 1/8 tsp of the chilli powder and 1/8 tsp of the powdered cayenne pepper.The pint should be frozen for 24 hours, on a flat surface in the freezer.
- Put the pint back in the freezer after 24 hours and turn on the Ninja Creami machine! Now is the magic time.
- Grab the Ninja Creami outer bowl after removing the pint's lid. Put the top on the outer bowl after securing the pint within. Once the cover is on, insert the outer bowl into the appliance and turn it until it locks in place by turning to the right. When the creamy delight appears, press the "Ice Cream" button and (try to) wait patiently.
- To remove the bowl from the machine after the procedure is complete, push and hold the button on the Creami's left side. Remove the pint by twisting the outer bowl's cover off.Your frozen Mexican hot chocolate is now ready for consumption!

NINJA CREAMI ORANGE CREAMSICLE ICE-CREAM

INGREDIENTS:

- Cream cheese, 1 tablespoon
- Orange extract, 1 teaspoon; vanilla extract, 1/2 teaspoon
- 1/4 cup Heavy Cream, 1/3 cup Granulated Sugar
- Whole Milk, 1 cup, a few drops of yellow and red food coloring (Optional)

DIRECTIONS:

- 1 tablespoon of cream cheese should be microwaved for 5 to 10 seconds in a medium bowl. The five to ten seconds in the microwave will assist soften cream cheese if it was in the fridge so that it can combine properly with the other components.
- 1/3 cup sugar, 1 teaspoon orange extract, and 1/2 teaspoon vanilla extract are combined with cream cheese. Mix the ingredients together by whisking.
- Whisk in 3/4 cup heavy cream and 1 cup whole milk gradually.
- Until the mixture is the desired hue, whisk add a few drops of yellow and a few drops of red food coloring.
- Making sure the mixture doesn't exceed the maximum fill line, pour the mixture into a Ninja Creami pint container.
- The pint should be frozen for 24 hours, on a flat surface in the freezer.
- Put the pint back in the freezer after 24 hours and turn on the Ninja Creami machine! Now is the magic time.
- Grab the Ninja Creami outer bowl after removing the pint's lid. Put the top on the outer bowl after securing the pint within. Once the cover is on, insert the outer bowl into the appliance and turn it until it locks in place by turning to the right. When the creamy delight appears, press the "Ice Cream" button and (try to) wait patiently.
- To remove the bowl from the machine after the procedure is complete, push and hold the button on the Creami's left side. Remove the pint by twisting the outer bowl's cover off.
- Your orange creamsicle ice cream is now prepared for consumption.

Made in United States
North Haven, CT
15 July 2023

39049955R00049